# BEAR RESCUE

# BEAR RESCUE

## Changing the Future for Endangered Wildlife

**KELTIE THOMAS**

FIREFLY BOOKS

A FIREFLY BOOK

Published by Firefly Books Ltd. 2006

First printing

PUBLISHER CATALOGUING-IN-PUBLICATION DATA (U.S.)
(Library of Congress Standards)

Thomas, Keltie, 1966–
Bear rescue : changing the future for endangered wildlife / Keltie Thomas.
[64] p. : col. photos. ; cm. (Firefly animal rescue)
Includes index.
Summary: Provides details and facts about bears from around the world, their endangerment and a range of conservation programs to save them, including profiles of individual conservationists and bear species.
ISBN-10: 1-55297-922-9 — ISBN-13: 978-1-55297-922-8
ISBN-10: 1-55297-921-0 — ISBN-13: 978-1-55297-921-1 (pbk.)
1. Bears—Juvenile literature. 2. Endangered species—Juvenile literature. 3. Wildlife conservation—Juvenile literature.
I. Title. II. Series.
599.78 dc22 QL737.C27T56 2006

LIBRARY AND ARCHIVES CANADA CATALOGUING IN PUBLICATION DATA
Thomas, Keltie
Bear rescue : changing the future for endangered wildlife / Keltie Thomas.
(Firefly animal rescue)
Includes index.
ISBN-10: 1-55297-922-9 — ISBN-13: 978-1-55297-922-8 (bound)
ISBN-10: 1-55297-921-0 — ISBN-13: 978-1-55297-921-1 (pbk.)
1. Bears—Juvenile literature. 2. Endangered species—Juvenile literature. 3. Wildlife conservation—Juvenile literature.
I. Title. II. Series.
QL737.C27T484 2006       j599.78       C2005-907371-3

Published in the United States by
Firefly Books (U.S.) Inc.
P.O. Box 1338, Ellicott Station
Buffalo, New York 14205

Published in Canada by
Firefly Books Ltd.
66 Leek Crescent
Richmond Hill, Ontario L4B 1H1

Cover and interior design: Kathe Gray/electric pear and Ingrid Paulson

Printed in China

*The publisher gratefully acknowledges the financial support for our publishing program by the Canada Council for the Arts, the Ontario Arts Council and the Government of Canada through the Book Publishing Industry Development Program.*

# TABLE OF CONTENTS

# THE BEAR FACTS

The sight of a bear standing on its hind legs is simply awesome. It turns the cute and cuddly image of the teddy bear on its head, and instead evokes fear and wonder. It reminds us a little of ourselves, standing on our own two feet. But above all, it embodies the untamed wilderness.

Bears amble through the wild as if it were a playground, safe from virtually all predators except humans. They pad through brush, nibble on tender young plants, swim in lakes and streams, and catch fish with their paws.

These mighty animals evolved from a long-extinct meat-eating mammal the size of a dog. This creature bounded through European forests 20 million years ago, and its descendants roamed far and wide around the world.

Today, the world's bears no longer rule the wild like they once did. Over the last 150 years or so, people have been moving into bear country, taking over vast chunks of wilderness, and forcing bears out. As people build houses, farms and cities, they destroy bear habitat. People also hunt bears for sport, and kill them for their body parts. The result? Populations of bears are seriously shrinking. Scientists now consider all species except brown bears and American black bears endangered or vulnerable.

But nobody's willing to count bears out just yet. Scientists, park rangers, governments, conservationists, and ordinary people around the world are working to save bears. What's more, bears have a nose for survival. What other creature can scare wolves into abandoning their kills so it can help themselves to their dinner?

---

< Grizzlies, once hunted almost to extinction, are now off the endangered list due to conservation efforts.

# WHERE DO BEARS LIVE?

Eight species of bear live in North America, South America, Europe and Asia:

**American black bears** (*Ursus americanus*) dwell in North American forests. Scientists estimate there are least 500,000 in the wild.

**Asiatic black bears** (*Ursus thibetanus*) live in southern Asia, northeastern China, eastern Russia and Japan. Estimates put the world population between 29,000 and 40,000.

The **giant panda** (*Ailuropoda melanoleuca*) is found in the alpine forests of China. It is one of the world's rarest animals, with just over 1,000 individuals in the wild.

**Grizzly or brown bears** (*Ursus arctos*) live in forests and mountains of North America, Europe, northern Asia and Japan. The total wild population is about 200,000.

About 22,000 **polar bears** (*Ursus maritimus*) inhabit the icy Arctic, which includes parts of Canada, the United States, Norway, Russia and Greenland.

**Sloth bears** (*Melursus ursinus*) live in grasslands and forests in India, Sri Lanka, Nepal, Bhutan and Bangladesh. Between 7,000 and 13,000 remain in the wild.

**Spectacled or Andean bears** (*Tremarctos ornatus*) live in the cloud forests of South America. Their population is about 18,250.

**Sun bears** (*Helarctos malayanus*) inhabit tropical rainforests of Southeast Asia, including Indonesia, Borneo and Malaysia. Scientists do not know how many are left in the wild.

9

# THE STORY SO FAR

**M**ost bear species aren't on the brink of extinction, but their numbers are drastically falling in many areas. Some populations have disappeared from their traditional habitats as human communities have grown and moved in on them.

∧ A sign at the entrance to Bridger-Teton National Forest near Cora, WY, warns visitors that they are entering bear country.

**3000 BC**   Populations of brown bears begin disappearing from Europe and North America as human beings encroach on their habitat.

**1700s**   Hunters seeking riches and adventure head to the Arctic to hunt polar bears.

**1800s**   The Atlas Mountain brown bear of North Africa and the Mexican grizzly go extinct. Brown bears also disappear from parts of Germany as human populations expand.

**1850s**   Records from Banff National Park in Alberta, Canada, reveal that the number of grizzlies is falling. The grizzly bear population of the western U.S., excluding Alaska, is estimated at 100,000. By the early 1900s, the arrival of European settlers will wipe out all but 1,000 in the United States.

**1900s**   Overhunting begins to threaten the world's polar bear population as airplanes, motor vehicles and telescopic rifles make the bears easier to hunt.

**1920s–'30s**   Brown bears disappear from California, Oregon, Arizona and the French Alps.

**1965**   Concerned scientists head to Fairbanks, Alaska, for the first international meeting on polar bears, whose numbers appear to be declining.

**1968**   The World Conservation Union (IUCN) forms the Polar Bear Specialist Group, an international group of scientists, to research and conserve the world's polar bears. Later, a Bear Specialist Group is formed to do the same for other species.

**1973** The world's polar bear nations—Canada, the United States, the Soviet Union, Norway, and Denmark (including Greenland)—sign a groundbreaking agreement to conserve polar bears. The agreement protects habitat and eventually reduces hunting to a sustainable level.

**1975** The Convention on International Trade in Endangered Species of Wild Flora and Fauna (CITES) calls for trade in polar bears and spectacled bears to be controlled to ensure the survival of both species. The U.S. lists grizzlies as a threatened species and gets a recovery plan underway.

∧ Measuring the size of a polar bear's head is no easy job. Researchers must temporarily sedate the great white bears first.

**1979** CITES calls for a ban on all trade of Asiatic black bears and sun bears.

**1982** The IUCN lists polar bears as vulnerable, one step away from being officially declared an endangered species.

**1989** Scientists estimate brown bears have lost more than half their range and numbers worldwide since the 1850s.

**1990** The IUCN lists Asiatic black bears, sloth bears and sun bears as vulnerable to extinction. CITES calls for a ban on all trade of sloth bears and brown bears in Bhutan, China, Mexico and Mongolia.

**1992** CITES calls for trade in all brown bear and American black bear populations to be controlled.

**1999** The Bear Specialist Group creates a conservation plan for each bear species to motivate people and governments around the world.

**2000** The Yellowstone population of grizzlies, estimated at fewer than 200 in 1975, has doubled or tripled. Grizzlies return to some areas where they had been wiped out for more than 40 years.

**2004** Scientists find that global warming is causing Arctic ice to melt. By 2100, they say there might be no summer ice left for polar bears to roam.

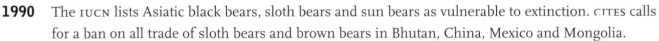

# WHERE THE BEARS ROAM

∧ A spectacled bear dines on leafy forest greens at the Columbian Nature Reserve.

Bears make themselves at home in a wide variety of habitats from the high Arctic to tropical rainforests, from mountain slopes to prairie grasslands.

Bears need large tracts of wilderness to survive. Individuals may have ranges as big as thousands of square miles. The only problem is, nowadays that often brings them into contact with human beings. Bears compete directly with humans for space, food and cover, and it's become a losing battle for the animals. Over the last 150 years, bears have lost more than half their territory to logging, farming and cities. As their habitat disappears, so do the bears.

To begin with, they may no longer be able to find enough food to survive. Bears are almost always hungry. One biologist who studied spectacled bears discovered that they spend 70 percent of their time eating. Bears wander through their home ranges dining on whatever is in season, and whatever they can get their paws on—grass, dandelions, cattails, fruit, berries, honey, nuts and salmon. They scavenge the remains of dead mammals and may hunt and kill newborn elk, moose and deer. Grizzlies can also take over and gobble up wolf kills by keeping the wolves away from the carcasses.

But even though bears are omnivorous—eating both plants and animals—most species mainly feed on plants. (One study showed that grizzlies in Banff National Park, Canada, eat a diet of 80 to 100 percent plants.) And that's exactly why bears are so hungry. They can't digest plant material very well, because they've inherited a meat-eater's digestive system from their ancestors. So they have to feed on huge amounts of plants to get the nutrition they need.

Grizzlies pack on the pounds before they hibernate in the winter. Some weigh twice as much in the fall as they did in the spring.

A bear's eating habits can get it into trouble in other ways, too. If bears wander into a logging camp or city in search of food, or if they raid livestock or crops for a meal, people often shoot them as pests, or as dangerous threats.

Finally, human activities break up bear habitat into pieces, or fragments. If bears have a tough time moving between these fragments because of these "roadblocks," bears may become isolated from others. This makes healthy reproduction more difficult and weakens the species' chances for survival.

# ATTACK OF THE CRAZY ANTS

Rhinoceros hornbills (*Buceros rhinoceros*) have developed an elaborate strategy for keeping snakes and other enemies out of their nests. Using material that she scrapes from the inside of the nest hole, the female seals herself into a tree cavity, leaving just a small opening through which the male passes food. When the chicks are seven weeks old, the female breaks out of the nest and the chicks reseal the entrance. Both the male and the female continue to feed the chicks until they are ready to leave the nest.

∧ Yellow crazy ants attack a land crab. The marauding insects have also driven birds from their nests.

Like the rhinoceros hornbill, many rainforest birds are amazingly well defended against natural predators. But they can be helpless in the face of unfamiliar species. When forests are logged, or cleared for farming or to build homes, predators move in. Domestic cats take a terrible toll on rainforest birds. So do rats and insects, which people may introduce unknowingly.

On Christmas Island, northwest of Australia, yellow crazy ants (named for their frantic movements) seriously threatened bird populations. Accidentally brought to the island more than 70 years ago, these ants became a problem when, for some reason, they suddenly began forming "supercolonies" that covered hundreds of acres. The ants forage mainly in the rainforest canopy and in these huge numbers are capable of driving birds from their nests.

The rhinoceros hornbill is helpless in the face of alien species, which can alter the structure of a rainforest.

Perhaps more seriously, the ants had begun to alter the structure of the forest itself by killing off red land crabs, which feed along the forest floor. More seeds began to germinate and the forest had begun to change dramatically.

Fortunately, a poisonous bait has brought the crazy ant problem under control, but it will be a while before the forest recovers.

"**P**lease look after this bear," reads the note attached to Paddington, the famous storybook bear from "darkest Peru." Nobody has to tell that to Armando Castellanos about Paddington's real-life cousins, the endangered spectacled bears of South America. The bear-tracking biologist is already on the case.

In 1999, in northern Ecuador, Castellanos started the Spectacled Bear Project. Its Spanish name is Espiritu del Bosque, meaning "spirit of the forest." The project's mission is to save spectacled bears—the spirit of the forest—and their forest home, which is being fragmented and destroyed by logging and farming.

It's a huge job. Castellanos and his team are reintroducing captive spectacled bears to the wild to help strengthen the population. They're also researching wild bears in the region. "Our goal is to determine the habitat use and home range of the spectacled bear," says Castellanos. "Very little is known about this elusive species. Spectacled bears are very difficult to study and capture in the wild. In the face of danger, they usually turn and run away or climb the nearest tree."

Nevertheless, Castellanos has managed to radio-collar and track several bears. Their findings reveal that the average home range of a male is more than 2,500 square miles (6,600 km²), which is several times larger than that of females. "It's virtually impossible to track males on foot in the same way females are tracked, because they travel long distances over rough terrain in a short time. I use a motorcycle to travel more quickly."

---

< The spectacled bear is named for the light-colored fur that rims its eyes and spans the bridge of its nose.

17

# VICTIMS OF FASHION

^ A spectator at the Royal Ascot horse races in Britain wears a hat decorated with a tropical bird feather.

Birds have one thing that distinguishes them from all other animals: feathers.

Feathers probably evolved from the scales of birds' reptile ancestors, and they serve many purposes. Birds are the best fliers in the world—better than insects or bats—thanks to their feathers. Feathers act as insulation, keeping birds warm in even the coldest water, and serve as camouflage, helping a nesting bird avoid detection by predators, for example. They are also important for display—the plumage of male birds, often more brilliant and patterned than that of females, attracts mates and warns off competitors, even predators.

Over the years the brilliant plumage of birds has attracted more than just the attention of other birds. Feathers have been used by people all over the world— in hats and headdresses, to make fans, arrows, fishing lures, pillows, quills for writing and many other items.

Our fascination with feathers has contributed to the decline of many birds. The now-endangered banded cotinga (*Cotinga maculata*), for example, was collected by people in Brazil for use in crafts. Though these striking birds are now confined to just a few protected areas in southeast Brazil, their blue feathers are still for sale on the Internet, where people buy them to make fishing lures.

These illegally exported parrot-feather ornaments were confiscated at the U.S. border.

Even one of the world's largest and most powerful birds of prey, the harpy eagle (*Harpia harpyja*) of South and Central America, is threatened by our desire for feathers. The eagle is an easy target because of its large size and boldness, and hunting is the most significant threat to this majestic bird. Its feathers are prized as symbols of power, and are coveted by local shamans and tourists alike.

# AT WORK | YOGANAND KANDASAMY

**F**riends call him Yogi—as in Yogi Bear. Yoganand Kandasamy has been studying sloth bears in India since 1996. Sloth bears, which have long snouts and three-inch (7.5 cm) front claws, were common where he grew up, though rarely seen. Most people feared them. But Yogi had a chance to study them in the jungle while at university, and he became fascinated by them.

∧ Yogi shares some face time with a sloth bear.

Yogi got to see sloth bears forage in their unique way, tearing apart termite nests to suck up the bugs with their snouts. He also got a close-up look at their scat. "I started wondering how these big bears could survive feeding mainly on such small things as the termites and fruits I found in their droppings."

Eventually, Yogi began researching the behavior and ecology of sloth bears by radio-collaring several bears and tracking them. "I followed them at all times of day to observe what they do: when they sleep, what they eat, where they get food, where they give birth, what they do when they meet a tiger, and so on. I put all this information together, like pieces of a jigsaw puzzle, to find out what a typical day in the life of a sloth bear is like." He also tried to rate the quality of the forest from the bears' point of view by determining how much area was covered by woodland and grassland, the number of termite nests, the number of fruit-bearing trees and shrubs, and the like. Because of his findings, people now have a good idea of what sloth bears need to survive.

20

Researcher Yoganand Kandasamy and an assistant radio-collar a sloth bear. Mission accomplished.

Loss of habitat is the greatest threat to sloth bears, says Yogi. If the bears' habitat can be conserved, so can the bears. Now Yogi is surveying sloth bear habitats throughout India to estimate population sizes and assess the threats bears face in each area. "Based on this survey, I will come up with a conservation plan for the bears. I'll probably be working on this for several years." It's a big challenge, but helping conserve sloth bears and their habitat is the part of his job that Yogi finds the most exciting.

Captured birds, like these in a Thailand marketplace, can spend weeks in overcrowded conditions before making their way to pet dealers around the world.

Once they've been trapped, the birds are transferred into baskets, boxes or bags and taken to the trapper's home, where they can stay for weeks or months in overcrowded conditions, often without enough food, water or light. Those that survive are flown to dealers and pet stores around the world. They don't all make it—for every bird bought as a pet, up to three others will have died during capture, in transit, or even in the pet shop.

Not surprisingly, many rare parrots are threatened because they're trapped for the bird trade. Some, such as the yellow-crested cockatoo of Indonesia and East Timor, are close to extinction. Others, such as Spix's macaw in Brazil, may already be extinct.

Conservationists are doing their best to control the trade in endangered birds. More than 160 countries have signed the Convention on International Trade in Endangered Species (CITES), a set of rules that aims to ensure that trade in wild animals and plants does not threaten their survival.

The illegal trade in wild birds may never stop unless the underlying causes are addressed. Poverty is a big one. Yellow-headed amazons sell for US$800 to $1,500, while a hyacinth macaw can fetch up to US$12,000, partly because only 2,000 to 5,000 remain in the wild. Though the person who actually traps one of these birds gets only a fraction of this amount, the money they make can equal six months' salary in some areas. Unless we find a way to do something about poverty in the countries these birds call home, the trade will continue.

∧ A sign in Costa Rica instructs people not to buy parrots from those who steal them from their nests.

# THE BEAR TRADE

The trade in bear body parts is worth a lot of money. Bear gall bladders have been used in traditional Chinese medicine (TCM) for thousands of years, along with bear fat, meat, paws, spinal cords, blood and bones. Conservationists report that on the black market gall bladders can be worth up to 18 times more than the equivalent weight of gold.

∧ One of these gall bladders can fetch a small fortune on the Asian black market. The gall bladder is the most prized part of a bear.

Ancient Chinese doctors wrote prescriptions for bear bile—fluid stored in the gall bladder—as far back as the ninth century. They used the bile to treat illnesses such as fever, hemorrhoids, sore eyes, liver disease and heart disease. The practice spread to Korea, Japan and Vietnam, and today TCM practitioners use bear bile the same way, throughout Asia and countries with large Asian populations, such as the U.S. and Canada.

As it turns out, those ancient Chinese doctors were onto something. Studies show that a chemical bears produce in their bile can successfully treat some liver diseases and dissolve gallstones without surgery. The treatment is so effective that people have developed inexpensive ways to make it without bear bile, as well as herbal remedies that can replace it. The problem is that many TCM practitioners do not believe that these alternatives work as well as bear bile, and so the illegal hunting continues.

In China, bear farms, where bears are held in cages and "milked" daily for their bile, have also sprung up to supply the great demand. At first, the Chinese government thought bear farming would protect wild bears, as people would no longer need to hunt them and kill them for bile. But that didn't prove true, because some TCM practitioners believe wild bear bile is more potent. What's more, with more bear bile available, more bile products have appeared, such as shampoo and wine.

An Asiatic black bear milked for bile from its gall bladder lives behind bars at a bear farm in China.

The good news is that some relief is on the way. Recently, wildlife organizations won the support of the Chinese government to rescue bears from bile farms.

Jill Robinson had heard about bear bile farms in China, but nothing prepared her for the first time she saw what went on behind the scenes.

∧ Jill Robinson greets a black bear in a transport cage at Pan Yu Bear Sanctuary.

In 1993, the animal rights worker went undercover on a farm tour to do some investigating. "I broke away from the group and found stairs leading to a basement below the farm," says Robinson. "The vision was shocking." She found 32 Asiatic black bears—called moon bears for the beautiful yellow crescents on their chests—held in metal "crush cages" that barely allow the animals to move. The bears were making nervous popping sounds, indicating their fear. "When I looked at their damaged bodies, I knew why they were afraid. They had been deliberately declawed and their canine teeth had been brutally hacked away to make them easier to 'milk.'"

Crude metal tubes leading to the bears' gall bladders poked out of infected holes in their bellies, revealing just how the farmer removed the bile, which would then be sold to be made into traditional Chinese medicines.

Just then Robinson felt something touch her shoulder. She spun around to see a bear with its arm stretched through the bars of the cage. "I took her paw and, surprisingly, she didn't rip my arm out, but simply squeezed my fingers. Our eyes connected for a moment, which crossed every barrier of species and understanding."

A worker uses a pole to move the sanctuary's new arrivals that show up from farms in the tiny confines of "crush cages."

The experience changed Robinson's life. It inspired her to create a campaign to rescue the more than 7,000 moon bears held on China's bile farms. Robinson exposed the farm's cruelty on TV and in newspapers around the world. People were outraged. The local government responded by closing the farm in 1995 and giving the bears to Robinson and a rescue team for rehabilitation. In 1998, Robinson founded the Animals Asia Foundation to spearhead China Bear Rescue. Then she began negotiating with the Chinese government, trying to put an end to bear farming. And she didn't let up.

In 2000, Robinson's efforts paid off. The Chinese government signed a groundbreaking agreement with Animals Asia Foundation to rescue 500 moon bears from bile farms and work together to end bear farming. By 2004, China Bear Rescue had rescued 139 bears and shut down 39 farms. "Our sanctuary in Sichuan Province, is bursting at the seams with happy, healthy bears who have put their miserable lives on the farms far behind," says Robinson. More bears were on the way.

Moon bears, still in their crush cages, arrive at the sanctuary on the backs of trucks. After years of abuse, many are violent, aggressive and fearful, but that doesn't stop the rescue team from swinging into action. They unload the bears, move them to quiet rooms and offer them water and fresh fruit. The team also gives them objects and activities, which encourage the bears to explore the world. "They get toys for the first time in their lives," says Robinson. "They get foliage and vegetation. You very quickly start to see a turnaround in their personalities."

After a few days, the team gives the bears a drug to sedate them and then cuts them out of their cages. Eventually, over several months, the animals are released into a bamboo forest sanctuary. "The bears run out each morning and afternoon into a bright, new and interesting day," says Robinson. That's because the team moves a variety of sights, sounds and smells through the sanctuary to stimulate the bears' senses. Sometimes they put out huge frozen treats or dog toys stuffed with jam or raisins. Other times, they hang plastic buckets filled with food, which the bears have to work at to get, or build straw mountains with food hidden inside for the bears to sniff out.

China Bear Rescue also works with the local community. For example, when a bear farm closes, the team gives the farmer money to start a new livelihood. The team also runs an education center and programs to spread the word. Whether they're working with bears or people, the team has the same goal: to end bear farming for good.

A moon bear goes after an apple hung in a tree by workers at the Moon Bear Rescue Center.

**W**hen new bears arrive at the China Bear Rescue center in terrible condition, Gail Cochrane doesn't get sad. "These bears are the lucky ones," says Cochrane, veterinary director of the center, which rescues bears from China's bile farms. "Under our care, at least 90 percent of them will survive and be released into a large forest enclosure where they can finally behave like reasonably normal bears."

Cochrane began rescuing moon bears in 1995, doing emergency care when the bears first arrived, giving them health checks and performing surgery to remove their damaged gall bladders. Today, she directs a team of veterinarians, nurses and others who ensure a good and happy life for the bears. "Normally, for the first month after a group of new bears arrives, everyone at the center works at least 12 hours a day, seven days a week, to sort them out, move the bears into safe cages, and perform emergency surgeries."

∧ Veterinarian Gail Cochrane gives an anesthetized bear a checkup at the Rescue Center.

The bears don't give them an easy time of it. "Wild animals are very good at hiding when they are sick, so sometimes it's difficult to tell if they have a problem." When the team suspects a bear is sick, the vets have to put the bear to sleep with drugs before they can examine it.

Once she's diagnosed the problem, the fun begins—trying to treat the bears. "You can't hand a bear a pill and ask him to eat it. Whenever a bear needs medication, we crush the tablets and add them to a tasty milkshake."

Play time at the Rescue Center.

Bears usually remain in the hospital area for six months. Once Cochrane thinks they're ready, they're released into a den and gradually mixed with other bears. "I decide who their friends are going to be. We mix bears into groups based on personality, such as nice small bears in one group, and large grumpy bears in another."

The bears then get access to an outdoor forest sanctuary where they have toys and climbing frames to play on. "The most exciting part is watching a bear go outside onto grass, seeing them playing with other bears and enjoying life for maybe the first time," says Cochrane. "Being able to make such a difference in these bears' lives makes it all worthwhile."

# THERE GOES THE NEIGHBORHOOD

**O**ver the last 150 years or so, humans have moved into bear country, where they've destroyed the habitat and forced many bears out of areas where they once lived.

"Bears can get into trouble in a hurry if they get access to people's food and garbage."

In Canada's Rocky Mountains, for example, grizzlies run the risk of being killed by oncoming vehicles or trains. "The bears like to be in the bottom of valleys," says research scientist Stephen Herrero, who studies grizzlies in the region. "But that's where major highways and developments are. So once the bears are there, they face competition with another very aggressive species—human beings." People often remove or shoot bears to protect their property and families.

"Bears can get into trouble in a hurry if they get access to people's food and garbage," says Herrero. Garbage is like the bear's equivalent of fast food. It requires no hunting, because the big stink makes it easy for bears to find, and it's available 24/7, all-year round. In fact, some bears have given up hunting and foraging altogether to dine at the local dump every day. And these trash eaters are really gaining weight: a recent study reveals they're a whopping 30 pounds heavier than their actively hunting and foraging cousins.

< Police and conservation officers remove a 130-pound sedated black bear from Calgary's city limits.

Human activity can run bears right off the land. When people use chainsaws and bulldozers to clear vast areas for farming, forestry or buildings, they leave the area uninhabitable for bears. As people extract oil and gas from the ground, they often disturb and destroy bear habitat. What's more, the roads and highways they build to access these areas may make bear country more accessible to hunters and land developers.

∧ Like all bears, a grizzly cub knows no bounds.

Human beings and bears occupy the same niche, or role, in the world's ecosystems. We compete for the same land to live on, the same plants and animals to eat, and the same water to drink. People are moving farther and farther into the wilderness, and conflict with humans has become a dangerous threat to bears' survival.

Even though most people are terrified by the thought of meeting a bear, bears usually leave the scene at the first sign of humans. Apart from polar bears, which have been known to prey on humans when no other food is around, bears are not man-eaters. They rarely attack people unless they feel threatened or are trying to protect cubs. However, if bears encounter humans frequently, they become used to them, and will start coming closer. If these bears get their paws on our garbage, they may start to link people with food and boldly approach humans. And before the bear realizes the danger, it may be shot dead.

Garbage dumps can become easy foraging grounds of "fast food" for bears.

"Once bears get rewarded for aggressively seeking out people's food and garbage, they usually have a relatively short lifetime," says Herrero. So if we want bears to survive, we need to ask ourselves how we can live alongside one another.

"**K**ill them all. They're too dangerous to live with."

When bear attacks killed two people in Canada's Glacier National Park in 1967, that's what some people were saying about grizzlies. But not Stephen Herrero. "Just how dangerous were grizzly bears, I asked myself, and what would it mean if they were all killed in areas like that?"

∧ Stephen Herrero (far right) and a team of researchers weigh a tranquilized bear.

A professor at the University of Calgary, Herrero decided to find out. He began researching the ecology and behaviour of grizzly bears, and over the years, he and other scientists have concluded that human beings are much more dangerous to bears than vice-versa.

Herrero has been impressed by people's change in attitude toward grizzlies. Nowadays, many people want to protect the bears rather than eliminate them, and their concern even funds his research. From 1994 to 2004, Herrero led the Eastern Slopes Grizzly Project to determine the effects of human activities on grizzly bears in the central Rockies. "It's one of the most developed landscapes in North America where grizzly bears survive. Much of it is just an hour or two away from Calgary, which has a population of one million people."

People use the area for recreation, tourism, drilling for oil and gas, cattle farming, forestry, and hunting—all of which can put bears into conflict with humans. People wanted to know how grizzlies were holding up under all this pressure. So Herrero and a team of researchers set out to find answers to the following questions: Was the number of grizzlies in the area increasing or decreasing? Which habitats did grizzlies prefer? What factors limited the bears' ability to survive?

They invited all the involved people in the area—from cattle ranchers, to oil and gas developers, to wildlife managers—to join them. "It was encouraging that these diverse groups came together to help support the research, listen to it, and try to apply it as we were finding it."

For example, as the research revealed which habitats grizzlies preferred, the oil, gas and forestry companies adjusted where they worked and built roads. Of course, not all conflicts between the companies and the bears worked out so nicely. "If there's $20 million worth of oil and gas sitting under an area that seems to be important habitat, bears don't always win," says Herrero.

Nevertheless, Herrero remains hopeful. "I think we've got a big enough chunk of wild land, and people care enough to maintain grizzlies at least 50 years into the future. By then, I hope we will have come to treasure them so much that we'll continue to take the extra steps needed to ensure their survival."

∧ A grizzly and her cubs hang out near the river's edge, where they are in reach of an easy meal such as salmon.

In the early 1980s, Carrie Hunt got tired of watching bears die. Whenever a bear was discovered lurking around human settlements to find an easy meal, it usually wound up dead. If someone didn't shoot it on the spot, biologists would try to relocate the bear by sedating it and airlifting it hundreds of miles away. Even then, the bear would almost always come back and have to be put down to ensure people's safety.

**Whenever a bear was discovered lurking around human settlements to find an easy meal, it usually wound up dead.**

So the Utah researcher and wildlife biologist decided to find a way to teach bears survival skills. She had heard that some people relied on dogs to keep bears out of their camps and ranches, so she went looking for a dog breed that could help teach black bears and grizzlies to stay out of human areas. What she found were Karelian bear dogs—a black-and-white breed that look like huskies. Karelians had been bred to hunt bears and other large game in Finland and Russia for years.

Carrie Hunt (right), Wind River Bear Institute staff, and these three Karelian bear dogs train bears to stay away from human settlements.

Hunt began training Karelian bear dogs to shepherd bears away from human settlements, much like collies lead sheep. In 1996, she founded Wind River Bear Institute to run problem bears out of town safely and teach them to stay away.

Wildlife officers release a 400-pound black bear found sleeping on a back porch in Palmer, WA, as three Karelian bear dogs bark and get set to give chase.

When a problem bear is discovered, it is trapped, radio-collared, then released at the scene. Hunt then yells "Get out of here, bear!" as other team members fire rubber bullets and bean bags at the bear's rump. All the while, the dogs bark ferociously and chase the bear away. Once the bear is back where it's safe and sound, the dogs give up the chase. Chances are the nasty experience will deter the bear from returning to the scene. Of course, that doesn't mean it won't become a problem elsewhere. That's where the radio collar comes in: it allows the team to anticipate where the bear might show up—and to make sure the dogs will be waiting. Eventually, the bear learns that looking for food in human settlements is more trouble than it's worth.

Even then, the Wind River Bear Institute's job is only half finished. Hunt and her team do just as much work with people, teaching them not to attract bears. They investigate the house or site to figure out what attracted the bear—often people don't realize that a bird feeder, unsecured garbage, pet food, compost pile or garden can lure the animals.

"No matter how much shepherding the team does," Hunt writes, "if people don't change their ways and don't clean up bear attractants, bears will continue getting into trouble." Her unique techniques are working. The lessons are proving to keep bears out of trouble in Utah, Montana, Washington and Alberta, and they're showing that bears and people can live together on the same turf.

^ A Karelian bear dog barks ferociously at a captured bear in a cage.

# SEALS FOR DINNER

The polar bear is the world's biggest meat-eating land animal, with some males weighing as much as a small car. It's a fearsome hunter that's uniquely adapted to its icy Arctic home, and its favorite food is baby ringed seal.

The polar bear's white fur coat enables it to stalk seals under the cover of ice and snow. As the lone hunter lopes across the sea ice, the soles of its feet work like suction cups to prevent it from slipping. The bear sniffs the air to catch the scent of a seal, or their breathing holes in the ice. Amazingly, a polar bear can detect the whiff of a breathing hole buried under three feet of snow from as far away as half a mile (1 km).

The bear then closes in slowly and quietly to catch the seal by surprise. If the seal is hanging out in a den above the breathing hole, the polar bear leaps up, crashes in, and slashes the seal to death with its claws. But if no seal is around, the polar bear will lie and wait for hours. The stealthy hunter may build a wall of snow and hide behind it. Then, when an unsuspecting seal surfaces for air, the bear may club it, flipping it out of the water with a single blow of its paw.

A hungry polar bear will gorge on the meat, blubber, skin and bones of its kill. But usually adult bears eat only the fat, which is rich in energy. Since ringed seal pups have lots of body fat, they make an especially satisfying polar bear meal.

< A polar bear hunts and kills a seal to dine on a blubbery meal.

# ON THIN ICE

The heat is on in the Arctic, and it's putting polar bears on thin ice.

Global warming is causing the Arctic sea ice to become thinner and smaller. The sea ice is breaking up about three weeks earlier in the spring, and freezing later in the fall. Polar bears depend on sea ice as a hunting platform to catch their main meal, the ringed seal, so the earlier breakup and later freeze shortens their hunting season. With such limitations polar bears may not be able to store up the fat they need to survive when the summer ice melts and forces them ashore for several months, until the freeze comes and they can hunt again.

Canadian polar bear biologist Ian Stirling has found that for every week that melts away from the spring hunting season, female polar bears in Churchill, Manitoba, step ashore 22 pounds (10 kg) lighter. With less fat tucked away, their health becomes poorer and they have fewer cubs. They also produce less milk to nurse the cubs they do have, and fewer young survive.

So what's cranking up the heat in the Arctic and nudging polar bears toward a meltdown? According to a major 2004 report by 250 scientists, fossil fuels are the culprit. As people burn coal, oil and gas for energy, carbon dioxide gets released into the atmosphere. The atmosphere traps heat from the sun on the Earth's surface like a blanket, and as carbon dioxide piles up, this blanket gets thicker and traps more heat. And the Earth gets warmer.

Warming in the Arctic is two or three times more dramatic than in the rest of the world. If the current trend continues, and people do not cut back on burning fossil fuels, almost all summer sea ice may disappear by 2100. Then the world's polar bears may become extinct—vanishing along with the ice.

---

If sea ice disappears due to global warming, the polar bear population may be headed for a meltdown.          >

# AN ARCTIC MESS

^ A toxic soup of chemicals from industrial plants all over the world build up in the Arctic.

The polar bear's Arctic habitat is hardly pure as newly fallen snow. The bears may live at the top of the world, but they're not beyond pollution's toxic reach.

Polar bears are exposed to a nasty mix of pollutants that winds and ocean currents carry to the Arctic. Pesticides and manufacturing processes in countries to the south can create toxic chemicals called persistent organic pollutants (POPS). These POPS, which have been linked to cancers and other health problems in humans and animals, take a long time to break down.

Arctic animals absorb and ingest the pollutants, which collect in their fat and vital organs. Then, as one animal eats another, the pollutants move up the food chain in increasingly high levels. By the time polar bears—the top predators in the food chain—sink their teeth into a meal, they ingest a concentrated wallop of pollutants.

Recent studies show that as the pollutants build up, the bears' levels of vitamin A and thyroid hormones go down. Vitamin A and thyroid hormones are important for growth, development, reproduction and fighting disease. Female bears can also pass high doses of the pollutants onto their cubs through breast milk. Sometimes the pollutants poison the milk and the cubs don't survive.

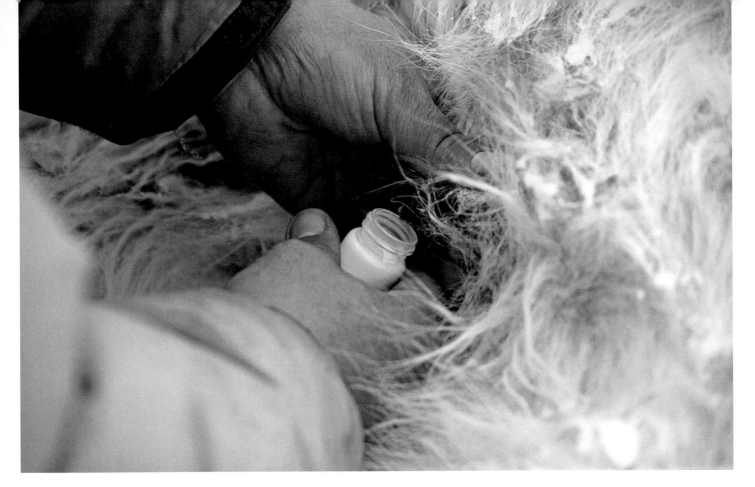

A researcher takes a breast milk sample from a polar bear near Resolute, Canada, to study it for toxins.

There is some good news for bears. Many of these POPs are no longer widely used, and conservation organizations are working to stop the use of similar chemicals around the world. So even though bears have to contend with the current mess, the situation may improve.

Ian Stirling has one cool job. The senior research scientist with the Canadian Wildlife Service treks through the Arctic studying seals—also known as polar bear chow—and keeps close tabs on the polar bears that live around western Hudson Bay.

Even after 38 years on the job, Stirling still finds it exciting to work with animals in truly remote wild places. "I love watching undisturbed polar bears hunting seals in the Arctic and marveling at how they have adapted to live in such a severe environment. While the Arctic is severe to us, it isn't to the bears. It's just a home for them, and a comfortable one at that."

∧ Research scientist Ian Stirling writes up notes from the field on Herschel Island.

During a typical day on the ice, Stirling gets up at 6:30 a.m., cooks breakfast in the camp, then hops into a helicopter to search for polar bears. He and his fellow researchers capture, tag, measure and release bears all day long until dark. They collect a small tooth from each bear to determine its age, hair to check for contaminants and a small fat sample to study the bear's diet. Then they return to camp, cook dinner, write field notes, preserve their collected specimens, and get set to do it all over again the next day.

Stirling and his research team are closely monitoring polar bears' reproduction and physical condition to determine how the bears are responding to global warming. Every year, the researchers check how much fat the bears are carrying and make other measurements that enable them to assess the animals' condition.

Ian Stirling removes a satellite collar used to track this polar bear.

As temperatures rise, the ice breaks up earlier in the spring and polar bears have less time to hunt and fatten up to get through the lean hunting time of summer. "The earlier the ice breaks up, the poorer the condition and reproduction of the bears. If the climate continues to warm as predicted, it doesn't look good for polar bears in western Hudson Bay in the next 30 to 50 years."

Maybe that's why Stirling isn't coming in from the cold just yet. He hopes to learn how climate change will affect areas farther north and help scientists develop conservation plans for polar bears and other creatures that live there.

# BEARS IN CAPTIVITY

Conservationists agree that protecting disappearing habitat is the number one priority for ensuring the long-term survival of all bear species. Nevertheless, zoos also play an important role in bear conservation. Many people may never encounter a bear in the wild, so seeing bears in zoos gives them the opportunity to learn about the different species and the survival risks they face.

The sun bears at Woodland Park Zoo in Seattle are like ambassadors of the species. "Each of these bears tells a special story," says Cheryl Frederick, the zoo's sun bear keeper and Species Survival Plan (SSP) coordinator. "They are telling the story of what's happening to bears in Borneo, which is what's happening to bears throughout all of their range countries." Woodland Park's sun bears come from rescue centers, where they wound up as former pets, orphans, and displaced wildlife whose habitat is disappearing.

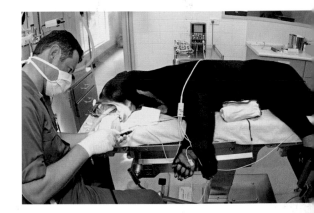

∧ A zoo veterinarian gives a sun bear a physical and dental checkup.

Zoos throughout North America work together to run Species Survival Plans for bears. They breed bears to try to maintain healthy and genetically diverse populations as "lifeboats" in case the species becomes extinct in the wild. The zoos also support wild bears by raising funds for field research and habitat protection programs. "We've supported a sun bear education center, field research, and formed expert teams, which are going to be the foundation of future conservation programs," says Frederick. "All that really comes back to having these bears at our zoo."

< Zoos give people the opportunity to see and learn about bears safely.

∧ Cheryl Frederick (left) meets Suntil, an eight-month-old orphaned cub, at a rescue center in Borneo.

In 2004, Suntil, a bear from Borneo at Woodland Park Zoo in Seattle, became the world's first sun bear to undergo artificial insemination.

The little bear's story begins in the 1990s, long before she was born, with scientists in the sun bear Species Survival Plan scratching their heads. Why had sun bears, the world's smallest and perhaps most endangered bears, never bred well in captivity? The North American captive population was aging and no one could figure out why they weren't reproducing.

In 1996, the ssp decided to start afresh by bringing 10 bears from rescue centers in Borneo to North American zoos. The only problem was that males were scarce in the rescue centers. "We wound up with nine females and one male, which does not make a breeding population," says Cheryl Frederick, the ssp's coordinator. "So in 2000, we went back over to get another 10 bears."

Suntil, the world's first sun bear to undergo artificial insemination, hangs out at the Woodland Park Zoo in Seattle.

This time they brought back five females and five males. One of those bears was Suntil, an eight-month-old orphan who went to Woodland Park Zoo. But even with the five new males, the captive female sun bears still outnumbered the males more than two to one. So the ssp rotated the males among the zoos. Each male spent a few years with a female at one zoo then moved to another to mate with another female. "It's kind of like a dating game," says Frederick. "You hope it will work out."

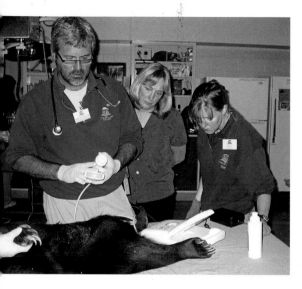

∧ Veterinarians artificially inseminate Suntil to try to breed sun bears.

Well, four years later, the dating game wasn't working out—only one cub had been born. The scientists worried that if the bears didn't start breeding soon, the North American captive population would die out.

Looking for answers, Frederick began to monitor when the bears came into heat and tried to better understand the reproductive biology of the species. "It's something that you can study in captivity that you can't easily study in the wild," says Frederick, though the findings may also be helpful for conserving wild sun bears.

Meanwhile, the SSP looked at other breeding options. Could sun bears reproduce through artificial insemination? This involves depositing sperm from a male into the uterus of the female in an effort to make her pregnant. There was only one way to find out: the SSP decided to try it on Suntil.

Woodland Park called in the experts from the San Diego Zoo, who had performed artificial insemination successfully on giant pandas, to lend their expertise. Frederick then watched Suntil for signs of estrus, or heat. Once she thought Suntil was close to ovulating, or releasing an egg, the San Diego Zoo vet hopped on a plane with frozen sperm from a male sun bear at her zoo. Then they used a small tube called a catheter to deposit the sperm into Suntil's vagina.

## "It's all about getting some baby bears."

After that, the waiting game began. Would Suntil become pregnant? Frederick and her colleagues gave Suntil weekly ultrasound tests to check, but after three months they had to conclude that she was not.

Nevertheless, Frederick sees the experiment as a success, because blood tests confirmed that they had accurately timed Suntil's ovulation. "We were very close. If we'd had more sperm, we would have been able to inseminate her two or three days in a row, which is much more like natural breeding." Next time, they want to inseminate a sun bear at a zoo where a male is on site.

"It's all about getting some baby bears," says Frederick. With a viable breeding program, she explains, there will be an even stronger commitment to doing something about the bears in Borneo. "We're only now just starting to mobilize for sun bear conservation efforts. We don't really know how many sun bears are left in the wild, but we know their forest habitat is rapidly disappearing. I think the next 10 years are going to make them or break them."

# THE FUTURE FOR BEARS

**M**ost experts agree that the future for bears will be decided over the next 10 to 20 years.

Today, Asiatic black bears throughout Asia, sloth bears in India, sun bears in southeast Asia, brown bears in Mongolia, Tibet, France, Spain and Italy, and spectacled bears in Latin America face the most serious threats to survival. Yet until recently, few or no conservation efforts have been in place for them.

In North America and western Europe, where conservation efforts have been intense, grizzlies are on the comeback trail. The polar bear population, too, while still threatened by climate change, has risen from less than 10,000 in the 1960s to at least 22,000 today. This good news is thanks to hard work by scientists, park rangers, government agencies and the public.

Since human actions pose the main threat to bears—destroying habitat, hunting, trading bear parts and killing bears who prey on our turf—people have a large role to play in ensuring bears' survival. The big challenge is for people to find ways to share land with bears and live alongside them.

If any animal can inspire humans to rise to the challenge, it's bears. Not only are bears a marvel to behold as they romp through the wild, but they play the same ecological role in the world as we do. By protecting natural ecosystems where bears live, we conserve the air, water, land, plants and animals—the very elements we both need to survive.

< A grizzly bear surfaces near Alaska. Only time will tell if bears around the world can keep their heads above water in the game of survival.

# FAST FACTS

| | |
|---|---|
| **Scientific names** • | eight species in the family Ursidae; four of the best known species (polar bear, brown bear, American black bear and Asiatic black bear) make up the genus Ursus |
| **Size** • | in sun bears, the smallest species, males are 10 to 15 percent larger than females; body length 48 to 60 inches (120 to 150 cm) |
| • | in polar bears, the largest species, males are 25 to 45 percent larger than females; body length in females 75 to 85 inches (190 to 210 cm), in males 95 to 105 inches (240 to 260 cm) |
| • | weight 60 to 145 pounds (28 to 65 kg) in sun bears, and 880 to 1,320 pounds (400 to 600 kg) in male polar bears, with the occasional individual topping 1,760 pounds (800 kg) |
| **Life span** • | about 20 to 30 years in the wild; 20 to 40 years in captivity |
| **Locomotion** • | like humans, bears walk with the soles of their feet flat on the ground, a method that allows them to stand up on their two hind legs |
| • | bears usually walk slowly; however, they can run up to 35 miles (56 km) per hour in short bursts |
| • | most species can climb trees and swim |
| **Hibernation** • | in cold climates, bears sleep up to seven months through the winter when food isn't readily available |
| • | bears sleep in dens made in caves or holes in the ground |
| • | they do not eat, drink, defecate or urinate, though this sleep isn't true hibernation, as bears do not lower their heart rate, body temperature, breathing rate or blood pressure, and they may wake up and emerge during warm periods |

**Senses**
- smell is a bear's most important sense; used to identify other bears, detect danger, and find food
- polar bears have a very acute sense of smell; they can detect the scent of prey more than 6 miles (10 km) away
- most species are generally thought to have poor vision, although scientists now debate this; polar bears, for example, have good depth perception that allows them to detect still objects on the snow more than half a mile (1 km) away

**Paws**
- hind paws are larger than front paws and make tracks much like human footprints
- paws have five toes that end in sharp, curved claws; the claws are used for catching prey and digging
- pads on the paws help bears regulate their body heat

**Teeth**
- most adult bears have 42 teeth
- except for polar bears (which are mainly carnivorous) and sloth bears (which are mainly insectivorous) bears have unspecialized teeth to handle their omnivorous diet: the canines are long; the carnassials (for slicing meat) are not well developed; the first three molars are usually missing or extremely small; the molars are broad with flat crowns for crushing

**Reproduction**
- adult bears are solitary except during mating season in the spring and early summer
- pregnancy lasts seven to eight months
- litter size can range from one to four cubs, but is typically two
- cubs stay with their mother for a year or two; females usually mate every couple of years
- cubs are born blind and hairless and nurse much like human babies; newborns are about the size of a chipmunk

# HOW YOU CAN HELP

If you would like to learn more about bears and the projects designed to protect them, contact the following organizations or visit their websites:

**Animals Asia**
*www.animalsasia.org*

584 Castro Street, PMB 506, San Francisco, CA, U.S.A. 94114-2594
Phone (888) 420-BEAR
An international organization helping to rescue and rehabilitate Asiatic black bears from cruel farming practices. Provides a kids' site, free email updates, and suggestions for how to help.

**Bears.org**
*www.bears.org*

Information about bear species and myths as well as an email discussion list about bear issues.

**Bear Trust International**
*www.beartrust.org*

P.O. Box 4006, Missoula, MT, U.S.A. 59806-4006
Phone (406) 523-7779
An organization working to conserve all species of wild bears and their natural habitats.

**International Association for Bear Research and Management**
*www.bearbiology.com*

A group of bear experts who work on research and conservation projects around the world. The site includes species fact sheets and well as the conservation status of bears.

**The Bear Den**
*www.bearden.org*

Fact sheets, information and games put together by the American Zoo and Aquarium Association and Bear Taxon Advisory Group.

**Ursus International Conservation Institute**
*www.ursusinternational.org*

Box 321, Lundbreck, AB, Canada  T0K 1H0
Provides education and information about what bears need to survive. Its website contains information about individual species, threats facing bears, and living with bears.

**World Wildlife Fund Canada**
*www.wwf.ca*

245 Eglinton Avenue East, Suite 410, Toronto, ON, Canada  M4P 3J1
Phone (800) 26-PANDA
WWF Canada is involved in bear conservation projects around the world. The website offers activities and tips on how to take action as well as an Adopt a Polar Bear kit.

# INDEX

## PHOTO CREDITS

*front cover:* © Heidi & Hans-Jurgen Koch / Minden Pictures
*back cover:* Courtesy of Ian Stirling
p. 2   © Paul A. Souders / CORBIS/MAGMA
p. 6   © Galen Rowell / CORBIS/MAGMA
p. 10  Michael Smith / Getty Images
p. 11  © Flip Nicklin / Minden Pictures
p. 12  © Kevin Schafer / Peter Arnold, Inc.
p. 13  Michael Giannechini / Photoresearchers / firstlight.ca
p. 14  © Staffan Widstrand / naturepl.com
p. 15  John and Karen Hollingsworth / U.S. Fish and Wildlife Service
p. 16  © Tui De Roy/Minden Pictures
p. 18  © Pete Oxford Photography
p. 19  © Pete Oxford Photography
p. 20  Courtesy of Yoganand Kandasamy
p. 21  Courtesy of Yoganand Kandasamy
p. 22  © Fred Bruemmer / Peter Arnold, Inc.
p. 23  © Raymond Gehman / CORBIS/ MAGMA
p. 24  © Joel Bennett / CORBIS/MAGMA
p. 25  © IFAW International Fund for Animal Welfare / Chris Davies – A. Lyskin – www.ifaw.org
p. 26  © IFAW International Fund for Animal Welfare / Chris Davies – David White – www.ifaw.org
p. 27  © Animals Asia / Kees Metselaar
p. 29  CP (Greg Baker)
p. 30  CP (Greg Baker)
p. 31  © Animals Asia
p. 32  CP / Calgary Herald(Bill Herriot)
p. 34  © NHPA / Andy Rouse
p. 35  © Sid Roberts / ardea.com
p. 36  Courtesy of Stephen Herrero
p. 37  © Michio Hoshino / Minden Pictures
p. 39  Courtesy of the Wind River Bear Institute
p. 40  AP / Wide World Photos
p. 41  Courtesy of the Wind River Bear Institute
p. 42  © NHPA / John Shaw
p. 45  © Thomas Mangelsen / Minden Pictures
p. 46  © NHPA / B & C Alexander
p. 47  © Flip Nicklin / Minden Pictures
p. 48  Courtesy of Ian Stirling
p. 49  Courtesy of Ian Stirling
p. 50  © Gabe Palmer / CORBIS/MAGMA
p. 51  James Morgan/Reuters / Landov
p. 52  Courtesy of Dr. Darin Collins
p. 53  Courtesy of Gari Weinraub
p. 54  Courtesy of Gari Weinraub
p. 56  © Kennan Ward / CORBIS/MAGMA
p. 58  © Mark Raycroft/Minden Pictures
p. 59 (t) © Ted Miller / Peter Arnold, Inc.
p. 59 (b)© Renee Lynn / CORBIS/MAGMA

# AUTHOR'S NOTE

I would like to thank all the scientists and bear specialists who generously took the time to contribute their expertise and knowledge to this book, especially Bernie Peyton, Armando Castellanos, K. Yoganand, Jill Robinson, Gail Cochrane, Stephen Herrero, Ian Stirling, Cheryl Frederick, Darin Collins, and the Wind River Bear Institute.